IELTS Writing Task 2:

Model essays and how to write them!

Mike Wattie
www.ieltsanswers.com
www.ieltsexaminer.com
www.checkessay.com

About the author

I have been teaching English as a second language for over fifteen years in Taiwan and Australia, in language centres and universities. I have also been working as an English examiner. My area of specialization is teaching students how to pass the IELTS exam. I particularly enjoy teaching IELTS because I find it challenging to teach students the necessary skills and strategies that they need to pass, and I also find that my students are highly motivated – this is a joy for a teacher!

Other books in this series

IELTS Task 1 Writing Academic Test

IELTS Task 1 Writing General Test

IELTS Speaking Test Preparation

Acknowledgements

I would like to thank those responsible for their help in completing this book. I sincerely thank Phil Biggerton for his time editing this book. I would also like to thank some of my faithful students, Nhi Phan, Andrey Polyakov, and Maria Gvozdeva, for providing valuable feedback on this book. Thanks to all my past students as well, for giving me the inspiration and desire to write this book.

Copyright

© Mike Wattie 2013
All Rights Reserved
No part of this book or any of its contents may be reproduced, copied, modified or adapted, without the prior written consent of the author, unless otherwise indicated for stand-alone materials.

Contents

1. Overview 6
    1.1. Sample question 7
    1.2. The three biggest mistakes when taking the IELTS writing exam 8
    1.3. How to Improve 9
    1.4. Task sequence for IELTS essay writing 10
2. **Grading of tasks** 12
3. **Comparing the three types of essays** 13
    3.1. Structuring the three types of essays 14
4. **Parts of the essay** 16
    4.1. Introduction 16
    4.2. Body 19
    4.3. Conclusion 21
    4.4. Planning your essays 23
5. **Opinion essay** 25
    5.1. Typical question words 25
    5.2. Task Analysis 26
    5.3. Planning your essay 27
    5.4. Steps in writing your essay 29
    5.5. Model essay version 1: somewhat agree 34
    5.6. Template for opinion essay 35
    5.7. Model essay version 2: totally agree 36
    5.8. Model essay version 3: Outweigh 37
    5.9. More sample questions of opinion essays 38
    5.10. Common mistakes 39
6. **Both sides and opinion essay** 41

6.1.	Typical question words	41
6.2.	Task analysis	41
6.3.	Planning your essay	43
6.4.	Steps in writing your essay	45
6.5.	Model essay 1:	50
6.6.	Template for a both sides and opinion essay	51
6.7.	Model essay 2: [based on the template on the previous page]	52
6.8.	More Sample Questions	53
6.9.	Common mistakes	55

7. Two question essay 57

7.1.	Sample question words	57
7.2.	Task analysis	57
7.3.	Planning the essay	58
7.4.	Steps in writing your essay	60
7.5.	Model essay one:	63
7.6.	Template for a two question essay	64
7.7.	Model essay two:	66
7.8.	More sample questions	67
7.9.	Common mistakes	67

8. Improving your score 68

8.1.	Common mistakes with task response	68
8.2.	Improving task response	72
8.3.	Common errors with cohesion and coherence	73
8.4.	Improving cohesion and coherence	75
8.5.	Common errors with vocabulary	77
8.6.	Improving vocabulary	79

8.7.	Common errors with grammar	80
8.8.	Improving grammar	81
8.9.	Reduce errors	84

9. Vocabulary for common topics 88

9.1.	Education	88
9.2.	Health	91
9.3.	Media,	93
9.4.	Technology	95
9.5.	Crime	97
9.6.	The environment	99

10. Useful linking words and phrases 101

1. Overview

Writing Task 2 is designed to test your ability to write an academic style essay. You must present the information in your own words as complete sentences within paragraphs. You are required to write over 250 words, and the task should be completed in about 40 minutes (both part 1 and 2 must be finished in 1 hour).

Types of Topics

There are many different topics for essays in the exam, but typical topic areas include: education, crime, media, technology, social issues, technology and the future, and the environment. In this case it makes sense to build up vocabulary in these key areas in order to have sufficient language to write an essay well.

You can see the vocabulary pages of my website for ideas:

http://www.ieltsanswers.com/IELTS-Vocabulary.html

Types of Questions

There are three main types of essay questions that are included in the IELTS writing exam. It is important to learn how to structure each of these types. Each of these will be described more fully in the sections that follow. Briefly, they are an opinion essay, where you are asked to give your own personal opinion on a topic; a both sides and opinion essay, where you are required to discuss both sides of an argument and then give your own personal opinion on the topic; and a two question essay, which involves responding to two different questions.

> *Tip!*
> **Read the task carefully and make sure that you clearly understand the topic and type of question before you start writing. This is absolutely essential to score well in the writing test.**

1.1. Sample question

WRITING TASK 2

(How long you should spend)

You should spend about 40 minutes on this task.

Write about the following topic:

> Some people believe that the fast pace and stress of modern life is having a negative effect on families
>
> *To what extent do you agree or disagree?*

(Topic) *(Question)*

Give reasons for your answer and include any relevant examples from your own knowledge or experience.

Write at least 250 words. *(How many words you should write)*

Note that most of the parts of the task are standardised. For instance, you are always advised to spend about 40 minutes on the task and you are always required to write at least 250 words. In addition you are always advised to include relevant examples from your own knowledge or experience. Note that this is not a requirement, and you do not lose marks for not giving examples. Giving examples is only one way of supporting your main ideas.

The only part that changes for each task is the part shown in larger letters in the box in the middle of the task [see above]. This consists of a topic and a question. The topic tells you what you need to write your essay about, and the question tells you what you must say about the topic.

1.2. The three biggest mistakes when taking the IELTS writing exam

I have graded thousands of papers for the IELTS exam. The purpose of this article is to tell you the three major mistakes that candidates keep making in order that you may avoid them.

The first problem is poor time management. About 30% of my students who write IELTS exams under timed conditions fail to complete both Task 1 and Task 2. In this case their score for Task Response (one of the four grading criteria) is reduced, and to make matters worse their score is penalized for being under length. Therefore, this is like a double penalty and so you should make sure you can write sufficient words for both tasks by controlling your time. This means 150 words for Task 1 and 250 words for Task 2.

The second problem is rushing to start the task without properly reading the question. Again, also about 30% of my students will write an essay that is off-topic, which again not only lowers their score for Task Response but also makes it difficult to score well in the grading category of Cohesion and Coherence because often the essay does not make sense to the reader who is looking for a response to the question. A common example of this is with a question like "to what extent do you agree or disagree." This requires YOUR opinion, and therefore saying things like "some people believe that…." is off-topic, unless you state whether you agree with them or not.

The final issue is the frequency of errors. Try to allow time to proofread what you have written. In order to get above a six for vocabulary you may only produce occasional errors in word choice, spelling and word formation. The biggest error is the singular/plural form of words, so always check your nouns and verbs to see if they should have an "s" ending. For a grammar score of 7 you must produce frequent error-free sentences. The most common errors are with articles (a, an, the), so look at each noun and think about whether it needs an article. In other words if you can proofread your writing and cut-down the number of errors you stand a better chance of getting over the 6 hurdle for vocabulary and grammar.

1.3. How to Improve

In order to improve and score well in the exam I recommend you focus on the following aspects:

1. Learn how the test is structured and graded

2. Learn skills to improve your answers

3. Practice skills

4. Do lots of practice tests. If you want to have your essay assessed by an experienced examiner and tutor visit this page: http://www.ieltsanswers.com/IELTS-Writing-Correction.html

5. Receive feedback on practice tests

6. Use the feedback to improve your answers

1.4. Task sequence for IELTS essay writing

In order to complete your essay effectively and efficiently within the set time and conditions of an IELTS exam you need to have a very clear and systematic approach to writing your essays. From my experience as an examiner and teacher I recommend the following approach. You may wish to modify this a little for your own personal style.

1. Read the Task.

This is a critical step that is often underestimated. Missing a single word in the instructions might result in an essay that doesn't focus on the topic. For instance if the topic is about *young people* and you only write about people in general then you will have a weak score for task response. I also suggest you underline key words. This will help you to focus on them and will also assist with the next step.

2. Rephrase keywords in the task instructions.

You need to rephrase the keywords that are given in the topic for two reasons. The main reason is because if you do not, the examiner will put brackets around the words you have copied from the task and these words will not be included in your word count. This may lead to your essay being under length. As well as this, you should rephrase the keywords to show your talent with vocabulary.

3. Establish the topic and the question type (there are three different types of questions).

You must focus on the topic and question to score well for task response.

4. Plan the structure of the answer

A good plan helps you to reduce the amount of time you need to write your essay and also leads to a suitable structure. If you structure your essay well you will score well for cohesion and coherence. As well as this it will be easier for the examiner to see the quality of your task response.

5. Write your answer

If you have made a solid plan then the writing stage will go more quickly and smoothly. Make sure you stick to your plan while writing. Also, do not think of additional points for your essay while writing. Instead, utilise all of your brainpower on writing correct sentences using correct language, so that you will have an essay that will score well for vocabulary and grammar.

6. Proofread your answer if time permits

If you have any time at all left at the end of your exam, you should use it to proofread your essay, so that you will have fewer errors with vocabulary and grammar. Focus on looking for the common mistakes you make with your writing. Common ones are errors with subject verb agreement, articles [a, an, the], and the "s" endings of words.

> *Tip!*
> **Making a plan saves you time when you write your report and ensures you cover all the key points using an appropriate structure.**

2. Grading of tasks

Criteria	Requirement
Task Response This criterion assesses how well you have focused on the topic and answered the question.	✓ write over 250 words ✓ satisfy all the requirements of the task ✓ cover all parts of the topic ✓ cover all parts of the question ✓ develop main points
Coherence and Cohesion This criterion assesses how well you have structured your essay, used paragraphing, and connected your ideas.	✓ sequence information and ideas logically ✓ use a range of cohesive devices appropriately ✓ use paragraphing appropriately ✓ Have a clear progression throughout ✓ avoid unnecessary repetition of information
Lexical Resource This criterion assesses your vocabulary in terms of errors and also ability to use more advanced language.	✓ use of vocabulary to allow some flexibility and precision ✓ use less common vocabulary ✓ awareness of style and collocation ✓ avoid errors with word choices ✓ avoid errors with word formation ✓ avoid errors with spelling
Grammatical Range and Accuracy This criterion assesses your grammar in terms of errors and also ability to use more advanced sentence structures.	✓ uses a mix of simple and complex sentence forms ✓ produce error-free sentences ✓ avoid errors with grammar and punctuation

3. Comparing the three types of essays

Key question words

Opinion	Both sides + opinion	Two question Essay
What is your opinion?	Discuss the advantages and disadvantages	What problem does this cause? What are some potential solutions?
Do you agree or disagree?		
To what extent do you agree or disagree?	Discuss the advantages and disadvantages and give your own opinion	Do you agree? What are some other solutions?
Do you think the advantages outweigh the disadvantages?	Discuss both sides of this argument and then give your own opinion.	What are the causes of this problem? What are some potential solutions?

Example question

Opinion	Both sides + opinion	Two question Essay
Computers are being used more and more in education and some say there will soon be no role for the teacher in education.	Computers are being used more and more in education. Some people say that this is a positive trend, while others argue that it is leading to negative consequences.	Alcohol abuse is becoming more and more common in many countries.
To what extent do you agree or disagree?	Discuss both sides of this argument and then give your own opinion.	What are some of the problems it causes? What are some of the possible solutions?

3.1. Structuring the three types of essays

Introduction

Opinion	Both sides + opinion	Two question Essay
Rephrase question Position = state whether you agree or disagree and the extent (how much):	Rephrase question "This essay discusses…"+ [both sides] and [opinion]	Rephrase question "This essay discusses…" + [question 1] and [question 2]

Body

Opinion	Both sides + opinion	Two question Essay
reason 1 reason 2 reason 3/concession (argument against your main opinion)	Side 1 advantages Side 2 advantages [Note: keep your opinion out of the body. It is only about what people in general may think.]	question 1 question 2

Final paragraph

Opinion	Both sides + opinion	Two question Essay
Restating of your position + summary of reasons	Your Opinion State that both sides are important/have merits State which one is more important/better	Summary of question 1 and 2

Essay Structure

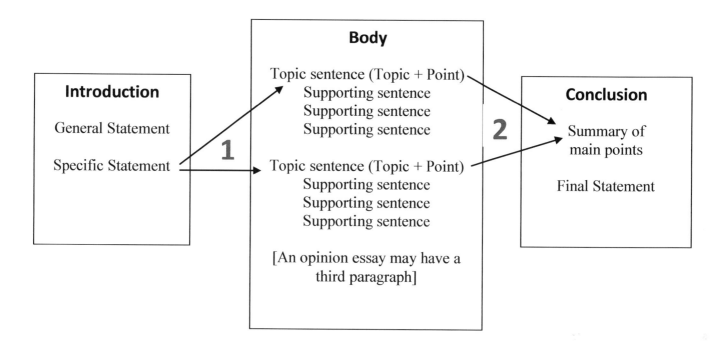

Point 1 above:

The diagram above shows how the last part of the introduction functions to influence the main points of each body paragraph. These main points are usually given in the topic sentence.

Point 2 above:

The diagram shows how the main points from the body get summarised in the conclusion of the essay

4. Parts of the essay

Further discussion is provided below on the structure of the essay, using the task below as an example:

> TOPIC:
> Computers are being used more and more in education and some say there will soon be no role for the teacher in education.
>
> QUESTION:
> *To what extent do you agree or disagree?*

4.1. Introduction

You only need two sentences for your introduction. You may have learnt from other teachers that you should include aspects such as a *background to the situation*, but you need to bear in mind that this is a very short essay of only a little over 250 words and so you want to keep your introduction brief. I suggest you just write a general statement and specific statement as explained below.

General statement

The general statement is the topic that you need to write about. You can write this very easily by just rephrasing the topic you are given. This is the best way to do this. Do not try to be creative here, as you will not be rewarded for this and you risk lowering your score for task response if you misstate the topic: with reference to the topic above:

> **Computers are being used more and more in education and some say there will soon be no role for the teacher in education.**

GOOD REPHRASE: *Some people believe technology may be used to replace teachers in the future.*

BAD REPHRASE: *Due to the rising prevalence of advanced technology computers are becoming more useful.* This misstates the topic because it is not about whether computers are useful it is about whether they will replace teachers.

Too long a rephrase: *Ever since the dawn of time, mankind has been finding ways to improve their lives. More recently education has emerged as a very important aspect of human lives. Therefore it is worthwhile to consider whether technology offers any advantages in the classroom and whether they are more useful than the people who have trained for many years as academic experts.* Too long! It is like a history lesson, and this also makes the topic a little unclear. If the writing is less clear then coherence is lowered. My key point here is that big long introductions do more harm than good. In addition, it is better to spend more time on the body of the essay, in order to show your ability to develop your main ideas which increase your score for task response.

Specific statement

The specific statement comes from the question part of the task. What you write will depend upon which of the three types of questions are asked. If the essay asks for your opinion you should give this here. If the question asks for anything else you should start this statement with this essay discussing and then rephrasing what you are asked for. Both of these approaches are explained further below.

<u>Specific Statement for an opinion essay</u>

QUESTION: *To what **extent** do you agree or disagree?*

This type of question needs to be responded to very precisely in the introduction. You need to have made a plan for your essay and have a clear idea of what your opinion is. To fully respond to all words in the question you need to mention the EXTENT or how much you agree or disagree. Some choices are:

> *Totally agree*
>
> *Somewhat agree*
>
> *Equally agree and disagree [this is a risky choice that I think should be avoided]*
>
> *Somewhat disagree*
>
> *Totally disagree*

So the sentence will look something like:

I totally agree with this opinion [good and safe choice]

I totally agree that teachers should be replaced with computers [better as there is a fuller sentence]

I totally agree that teachers should be replaced with computers because they are cheaper and more convenient for students [best because it gives the examiner a clear idea of what the essay is about. Paragraph 2 should be about cheaper, and paragraph 3 should be about being more convenient].

<u>Specific Statement for a non-opinion essay</u> = "**this essay discusses**" + **rephrase** of the question

QUESTION: Discuss the advantages and disadvantages of using computers in the classroom.

This essay discusses *the merits and drawbacks of the use of computers in schools.*

QUESTION: What are some disadvantages of using computers in the classroom? What are some ways to overcome these disadvantages?

This essay discusses *drawbacks with the use of computers in schools and also some ways to solve them.*

4.2. Body

The body of the essay should logically fit with the introduction you gave for the essay. The specific statement [last sentence of the introduction] should serve as a guide for the body of the essay. For instance, if you said you totally agree in the introduction then the body should consist of two or three paragraphs about why you agree. If you said you somewhat agree then the body should be mostly about why you agree, but also have a concession, which means that you are pointing out some arguments from the opposing side of your main opinion. The body of an IELTS essay should usually consist of two or three paragraphs. You need to have logical paragraphing to score well for cohesion and coherence.

Structure of the body of an essay

Opinion essay	Both sides and opinion	Two question essay
Reason 1 for opinion	Side A	Question 1
Reason 2 for opinion	Side B	Question 2
Reason 3 for opinion [optional]	[Opinion is given in the concluding paragraph]	

The structure of each paragraph needs to be logical and there should be ONE clear focus for each paragraph. The best way to achieve a clear focus and to communicate this to the examiner is by making this clear in the first sentence of each paragraph. This first sentence is called the topic sentence. Topic sentences usually have two key parts, which are the topic of the essay and the key point that this paragraph will discuss about this topic.

Topic sentence = topic + key point about the topic

Some examples of topic sentences relating to the previous task: **QUESTION: Discuss the advantages and disadvantages of using computers in the classroom.**

There are several merits of the use of computers in schools.

topic = *use of computers in schools*

key point about the topic = *merits*

However, there are some important <u>drawbacks</u> with using computers in education.

topic = *using computers in education*

key point about the topic = *drawbacks*

The first sentence of each paragraph, often referred to as a topic sentence, introduces the paragraph by stating and summarising the main point being made in the paragraph. Topic sentences often contain transition signals, which aid in the smooth transition from one paragraph to the next. This first sentence should inform the reader of the point you are making and how this paragraph relates to the question. In fact, if the reader were to scan your topic sentences, they should be able to obtain a sketch of the entire essay. This sketch should show the logical progression of the points you are making. The absence of topic sentences leaves the reader wondering what you are trying to say and why, ultimately confusing the reader. Signposting is not limited to topic sentences. Signposting within your paragraph also aids the reader. The following example illustrates the effective use of signposts (signposts are underlined).

<u>Finally</u>, as with all models of learning, rote memorisation has limitations. <u>For example</u>, the model implies that learning occurs in a serial processing form, whereas we know that learning is a recursive process. <u>Furthermore</u>, the model fails to take into account motivation, and social interaction as essential aspects of the learning process. <u>Nevertheless</u>, the model gives educators many useful guidelines for considering how information can be structured to facilitate learning.

Effective paragraphs have three important qualities.

UNITY: A paragraph should focus on one main idea.

DEVELOPMENT: this occurs when the idea is elaborated on in the paragraph. This elaboration usually consists of explaining the key point adding details about it or giving an example to illustrate it.

COHERENCE: This means everything in the paragraph should relate to and expand on the point you are making.

4.3. Conclusion

Given that an IELTS essay is only a little over 250 words and you have limited time to write your essay. It is important that you can write a brief but complete conclusion to your essay.

You need to send a SIGNAL to the examiner that you are making the conclusion to your essay. I like the phrase *in conclusion* best. I suggest you just use this as it can be used for ALL THREE types of essays. The more you can avoid the need to have to remember and correctly apply different phrases for each type of essay the better. I really hate *in a nutshell*. I think other people may hate this, so I don't recommend it. It is not impressive; I feel it is a cliché, or an overused phrase. I also don't feel it is formal. If you say *in summary* or *to summarise my main points* you will have to not use these phrases with certain types of essays. For instance, with a both sides and opinion essay you are not really summarising your main points in the final paragraph, you are giving your own opinion.

After the signal we have to apply two different structures depending on the type of essay. We can separate these into two types, an opinion for a *both sides and opinion essay* and a summary for an *opinion essay* or *two question essay*.

Conclusion for each type of essay

Opinion essay	Both sides and opinion essay	Two question essay
1. Restate whether you agree or disagree and also the extent. If your position is somewhat agree/disagree then make sure you put the side you support most first. 2. Summarise the main reasons for your opinion [summarise the main reasons from the body of your essay]. 3. Say something more. Ideally if you still have time try to write one more sentence to give a final opinion or recommendation based on your summary. This is the difference between a good conclusion and an excellent one!	1. State that both sides of the argument are important/have merits 2. State which one is more important/better 3. Say why. Justify your selection. This is the key to reaching grade 7 and above for task response. Remember that YOUR opinion is one of the three parts of the question and although this paragraph may be briefer than the body paragraphs it is a very important one.	1. Summarise the main points of question 1 2. Summarise the main points of question 2.
In conclusion, I totally disagree that machines can replace teachers. This is because teachers can encourage students to learn and teach them how to interact with other people.	*In conclusion, I believe both sides of the argument have their merits. On balance, however, I tend to believe that the advantages of studying using a computer outweigh those made possible by a teacher. This is because it is cheaper and more convenient to study online.*	*In conclusion, the main problems with using computers in schools are that students get distracted from studying and they use them to access inappropriate content. These can be overcome by educators monitoring their students closely and by restricting the websites they can access.*

4.4. Planning your essays

On a few occasions I have been an invigilator (person to make sure no one is cheating!) in the writing exam. I was amazed to see that about 10% just started writing their essays without writing any plan first. Afterwards, I asked some of my students who were attending why they didn't write a plan. "Oh we thought we didn't have time to do it."

The plan serves three purposes. First, it helps you think about the main points you will write, so it increases your score for Task Response. Second, it helps you structure your essay better, so it increases your score for Cohesion and Coherence. Finally, it saves you time. That's right! By making a plan first, you won't have to keep stopping to think what you will write next.

Each essay question is composed of two parts. The TOPIC, which is what the essay is about; and the TASK, which is what sort of essay you need to write. There are three main types of essays. The first asks your opinion, or do you agree or disagree. The second asks you to explain two sides of an argument and then give your own personal opinion on that topic. The third asks you two questions; for example, "discuss the problems and solutions."

You should learn how to plan for all three types of essays. You can practice your planning by looking at past exam questions and thinking what would be your main points and how would you structure the essay. If you need someone to correct your essays and give feedback on how to improve checkout my service at: http://ieltsanswers.com/IELTS-Essay-Correction.html

Tasks that include examples

If the task mentions "for instance" or "for example", that means you don't have to specifically mention those items. So you don't have to talk about sport or music you could talk about art instead

It is generally believed that some people are born with certain talents, <u>for instance for sport or music,</u> and others are not. However, it is sometimes claimed that any child can be taught to become a good sports person or musician.

Discuss both these views and give your own opinion.

Tasks that include two parts [usually signalled by "and"]

For the task below, the topic includes two parts and both must be referred to in the body of the essay. These two parts are cheaper and easier. You need to include both to get to 6 for task response and you need to cover both of them well to get to 7 and above.

These days, due to advances in technology, it is <u>cheaper</u> and <u>easier</u> to travel abroad.

Do the advantages outweigh the disadvantages?

5. Opinion essay

This type of essay tests your ability to state an opinion on an issue and then support it with logical reasons. To score well you need to explain your reasons clearly and use examples to illustrate the key points you are trying to make.

5.1. Typical question words

What is your opinion?

Do you agree or disagree?

To what extent do you agree or disagree?

Do the advantages outweigh the disadvantages?

To what extent do the advantages outweigh the disadvantages?

Sample task

> Some people believe that the fast pace and stress of modern life is having a negative effect on families.
>
> *To what extent do you agree or disagree?*

5.2. Task Analysis

It is important to realise that every task contains a topic and a question. You must fully address both the topic and the question to score six and above for task response. An analysis of the topic and question is provided below:

Topic: Some people believe that the **fast pace** and stress of modern life is having a negative effect on families.

Whenever you see the word **and** in the topic you must address both parts of this question. In this case the essay must address both the fast pace and stress of modern life in order to reach six and above for task response. Failure to address both parts of the topic results in a task response of five or below. This is because not all parts of the topic have been addressed.

Question: *To what extent do you agree or disagree?*

The question also has two requirements. You must state whether you agree or disagree and also the extent, or how much, you agree or disagree. In order to score a six and above you need to clearly state your response to the question including the extent to which you agree or disagree. In order to make your opinion clear I believe it is best to give your opinion in both the introduction and conclusion of the essay. Do not forget to mention the extent! Even if the question does not ask the extent, for instance it just asks do you agree or disagree, I still believe it is a good idea to state the extent. You can give the extent using words like totally or completely if you 100% agree or disagree; or somewhat or partly, if you do not fully agree or disagree. I strongly urge you to not 50-50 agree and disagree. This usually ends up being unconvincing and unclear.

5.3. Planning your essay

1. Underline key <u>vocabulary</u> in the topic and write words with the same or related meaning.

Some people believe that the <u>fast pace</u> and <u>stress</u> of <u>modern life</u> is having a

high-speed   pressure   contemporary lifestyles

<u>negative</u> <u>effect</u> on <u>families</u>.

harmful influence family life

2. Decide what kind of response is needed.

To what <u>extent</u> do you agree or disagree? = *say how much you agree or disagree*

3. Brainstorm key points for the answer.

Agree with negative effect on families	Disagree with negative effect on families
Fast pace leads to less time for families to be together	Due to the increased time pressure and stress families are forced to cooperate more, which brings them closer together
Stress leads to arguments among family members	

4. **Decide on your position** (totally agree, somewhat agree, somewhat disagree, totally disagree)

You do not need to give arguments for both sides of the topic. It is up to you, as it is your opinion. Rather than thinking about your real opinion, I suggest you look at the points you have brainstormed for each side of the argument, and then choose a side that you think will be the easiest to explain, and for which you have the better language to use. Remember this is a language test and not a test of your knowledge. The key point is to focus on language and structuring your whole task well.

5. **Decide on the structure of the essay**

Based on your position (extent you agree or disagree) put numbers next to each of the points you have brainstormed above in the order you will cover them. You should always cover the side you support more strongly first in the body of the essay. Also, you should always organise your points from strongest and weakest.

5.4. Steps in writing your essay

Once you have written a solid plan for your essay, you can begin the task of actually writing the essay. Having a good plan will speed up this process and ensure that you are consistent with your opinion throughout the essay. What I mean here is that the opinion you give in the introduction will fit the body of the essay, and the conclusion will restate the same opinion you gave in the introduction and summarise the body of the essay. If you achieve this high level of fit, you are likely to score well for task response and cohesion and coherence.

WRITING THE INTRODUCTION

1. Paraphrase the question

Given that you have already rephrased the keywords of the topic, in the planning stage, this step should be relatively easy. When you do write this sentence, in addition to rephrasing words also try to rearrange the order of words in the sentence. This may necessitate changing some of the word forms. For instance you might have to change nouns into verbs. This shows the examiner your ability to use language flexibly and can increase your score for vocabulary and grammar.

> Some people believe that the <u>fast pace</u> and <u>stress</u> of <u>modern life</u> is having a <u>negative</u>
>
> *high-speed   pressure contemporary lifestyles*
>
> *harmful*
>
> <u>effect</u> on <u>families</u>.
>
> *influence family life*
>
> *Many people feel that family life is being harmed by the high-speed and pressure of contemporary lifestyles.*

2. State your position [totally/strongly/somewhat + agree/disagree]

it is important to state your position in the introduction of the essay because it makes it clearer for the examiner what your position is and also when the examiner reads the body of your essay they already have an overall idea of what your essay is about. Then, in the likely event that you have errors with vocabulary and grammar they may be less serious because the examiner will have more of a context in order to guess the meaning of what you are trying to express. You can simply state your opinion, and this may be best if you only need a score of around six or seven and you struggle to finish your essay on time. However you can state your opinion and also the reasons. If you are trying to get to 8 I believe it is better to state both your opinion and the reasons. Although this will slightly increase the word length, this adds to the quality of your introduction, and also assists your task response as the introduction and conclusion of your essay are considered as important in establishing a clear task response.

I somewhat agree with this opinion because the fast pace leads to less time for families to be together, stress leads to arguments among family members; however, due to the increased time pressure and stress families are forced to cooperate more, which brings them closer together.

[I realise this is quite long and it may be beyond some writers. This is why a sentence of this quality can enable a candidate to get to level eight or nine]

BODY

After you have written the introduction, you will need two or three body paragraphs. For this type of essay, I suggest putting only one reason in each paragraph. A good paragraph should only have one main idea. You may write only two paragraphs if you are a person who likes to explain things in detail and use illustrative examples. If you prefer, you can write three shorter paragraphs. Whether you write two or three paragraphs may depend on the question and also the quality of points you have brainstormed. Personally, I would use three paragraphs if I were writing about both sides of the argument. This is because it is safest to have two paragraphs for the side you support more strongly and only one paragraph for the side you support less. This structure ensures your opinion is supported well, and prevents the risk of the body of the essay not matching your opinion. What I mean here is that sometimes someone says they somewhat agree, but then go on to argue more strongly about why they disagree. This sends both your task response and coherence and cohesion tumbling down!

1. Write topic sentences for each body paragraph

Each body paragraph should start with a topic sentence. For this type of essay the topic sentence consists of three parts, which are the sequencing word, topic, and reason to support the opinion.

Sequencing word + topic + **reason**

The main reason why I believe family life is being compromised **is because families have less time to be with each other**.

2. Write supporting sentences for the topic sentences

You can think of the topic sentence you have just written as being the introduction for the paragraph. It introduces the reason for your opinion, which forms the key point for the paragraph. Having a clear key point for the paragraph makes it easy for the examiner to understand what you are saying in the paragraph. In addition, if the key point of the paragraph is clear any errors with vocabulary or grammar will be less likely to prevent communication. This is because the examiner will have more of a context to guess any parts that are unclear. After you have written the topic sentence, you should support it by developing the key point. There are three ways to develop your key point: Explanation, example, adding details

Explanation: *As individual family members are busier at work and with their social lives they have less time to spend with their family.*

Adding details: *As well as this, people have many things they have to do these days such as checking e-mail, updating their online social status and so less time is left for family life.*

Example: *To illustrate, I spend about two hours online every night attending to daily correspondence before chatting with my family members, whereas ten years ago I would spend time with my family from the moment I walked in the door.*

[The example above could just consist of the first sentence. However, to fully make the point the second sentence is needed. This is the difference between a level 6 writer and a more competent writer.]

CONCLUSION

In order to write an excellent conclusion, you should start by using a phrase that signals you are concluding your essay. Then, you should restate the position to reinforce it in the mind of the examiner. After this you should summarise the main points you made in the body of the essay because this is a standard feature of a concluding paragraph and also it will remind the examiner of your key points and make your opinion more persuasive. Finally if you want to write a truly outstanding conclusion, and you have enough time, you could give a final comment based on your summary. If you are short of time just try to complete as many of the steps below that time permits. Note that if you are aware you are running out of time when writing the body of the essay, try to finish the body quickly and at least write something for this paragraph. If you do not have some sort of concluding paragraph the essay will be incomplete and the examiner may penalise you for cohesion and coherence. It will also make it difficult to get a high score for task response because the concluding paragraph is an important factor in assessing the task response.

Send a signal you are concluding your essay

I like *in conclusion*. This is a universally accepted way to finish an academic essay. There are other choices but this works well and can be used for all three types of essays. Some students think it is boring to use this phrase. However, keep in mind there are no marks for creativity and flair. You are not doing creative writing; instead you are taking a language exam. Every time I read phrases like *in a nutshell*, I am not impressed; in fact, the word yuck comes to mind! You can use phrases like *to summarise;* the reason why I'm against these is because they do not fit my structure for a both sides and opinion essay (for that essay the final paragraph will be your opinion and not a summary). I believe it is better to have a standard phrase that you can use for all three essays to avoid the need to remember different ones and to correctly applied them under pressure in the exam.

Restate your position

You should restate your opinion along with the extent. This is good essay writing. This is the way it's done. Many students don't want to do this and feel they have already said it, so they don't want to say it again. Up to you! I believe you should restate your opinion.

I somewhat believe that the rapid pace and stressful nature of contemporary lifestyles are having negative consequences on family relationships.

Summarise the main points

If you have time it is very helpful for your task response to summarise the reasons for your opinion. Note that you should ideally use different words and phrases than in the body of your essay. If you do this well it can increase your score for vocabulary because it shows the examiner your range of vocabulary.

This is because family members have less time, and when they are together they feel less relaxed. However, I admit that sometimes adversity can bring people closer together.

Give your final opinion or recommendation/ restate your position

If you have time, based on a summary, give your final opinion or make a recommendation. This is a way to really show the examiner your talent and reach a score of 8 or 9 for task response. This will really impress the examiner as it will show your understanding of what you've written and your ability to make further comment on it. This is a high-level language function.

Given this situation it seems that family members should try to be more supportive to one another and also parents need to set aside regular times for families to relax together.

5.5. Model essay version 1: somewhat agree

> Some people believe that the fast pace and stress of modern life is having a negative effect on families.
>
> To what extent do you agree or disagree?

Many people feel that family life is being harmed by the high-speed and pressure of contemporary lifestyles. <mark>I somewhat agree with this opinion</mark> because the fast pace leads to less time for families to be together, and stress leads to arguments among family members; however, due to the increased time pressure and stress families are forced to cooperate more, which brings them closer together.

<u>The main reason why I believe</u> family life is being compromised is because families have less time to be with each other. As individual family members are busier at work and with their social lives, they have less time to spend with their family. As well as this, people have many things they have to do these days such as checking e-mail, updating their online social status and so less time is left for family life. To illustrate, I spend about two hours online every night attending to daily correspondence before chatting with my family members, whereas ten years ago I would spend time with my family from the moment I walked in the door.

<u>In addition,</u> the pressure of life these days means that even when families do get together arguments are more likely. This is because everyone feels tired and they are more likely to get irritated and to react to their heightened emotional levels.

<u>However,</u> it does seem reasonable that this pressure may also lead to positive outcomes. One such possibility is that family members will cooperate more in order to overcome time limitations. For instance, they may share household chores, so that everybody has time to relax afterwards.

<u>In conclusion,</u> <u>I somewhat believe</u> that the rapid pace and stressful nature of contemporary lifestyles are having negative consequences on family relationships. This is because family members have less time, and when they are together they feel less relaxed. However, I admit that sometimes adversity can bring people closer together. Given this situation, it seems that family members should try to be more supportive to one another and also parents need to set aside regular times for families to relax together.

Comments about the previous model essay

You may have noticed that the previous essay was rather long. It was about 340 words. This is because of a high level of paragraph development in paragraph 2. Paragraph development can increase the score for task response and also cohesion and coherence. However, if we do a lot of paragraph development we should consider having fewer paragraphs. The following model has only two body paragraphs. In addition, it only covers one side of the argument [totally agree/disagree]. I believe this is a better approach because it is more persuasive and there is less risk that when you cover the other side of the argument you end up contradicting what you have previously said. It also means that your introduction and conclusion will be shorter because there are fewer things you have to mention.

5.6. *Template for opinion essay*

The template below has been used to write the second version of the essay.

Introduction

There is currently a contentious argument over whether XYZ [XYZ is the topic]

I totally agree/disagree with this opinion because [reason 1 + reason 2]

Paragraph 2

The main reason why I believe/don't believe XYZ is because... [reason 1]

Paragraph 3

Another reason why I support/don't support the notion that XYZ is due to the fact that... [reason 2]

Conclusion

In conclusion, I completely agree/disagree that XYZ because [rephrase reason 1] and [rephrase reason 2].

Given this situation, it seems that [give a final recommendation or opinion]

5.7. Model essay version 2: totally agree

> Some people believe that the fast pace and stress of modern life is having a negative effect on families.
>
> To what extent do you agree or disagree?

There is currently a contentious argument over whether family life is being harmed by the high-speed and pressure of contemporary lifestyles. *I totally agree with this opinion because* the fast pace leads to less time for families to be together, and stress leads to arguments among family members.

The main reason why I believe family life is being compromised is because families have less time to be with each other. This is due to family members being busier at work and with their social lives. As well as this, people have many things they have to do these days such as checking e-mail, updating their online social status and so less time is left for family life. *To illustrate*, I spend about two hours online every night attending to daily correspondence before chatting with my family members, whereas ten years ago I would spend time with my family as soon as I walked in the door.

Another reason why I support the notion that families are being impacted negatively is that the pressure of life these days means that even when families do get together arguments are more likely. This is because everyone feels tired and they are more likely to get irritated and to react to their heightened emotional levels.

In conclusion, I completely agree that the rapid pace and stressful nature of contemporary lifestyles are having negative consequences on family relationships. This is because family members have less time, and when they are together they feel less relaxed. *Given this situation, it seems that* family members should try to be more supportive to one another and also parents need to set aside regular times for families to relax together.   [281 words]

5.8. Model essay version 3: Outweigh

> Many people believe that the government should encourage industries and businesses to move from large cities to the countryside.
>
> Do you think that the advantages outweigh the disadvantages?

Nowadays, there is a contentious issue regarding whether the authorities should provide incentives for factories and other companies to relocate from metropolitan areas to rural sites. In my opinion the merits outweigh the drawbacks.

There are considerable benefits to locating companies in regional areas. For businesses themselves they can have a significant decline in costs, such as the leases on premises, which are usually dramatically higher in the big cities. It is also likely to benefit rural communities by boosting their economies and providing job opportunities in the neighbourhood and preventing the need for them to make a long commute to work in the city. Finally, by locating businesses in remote areas it can benefit cities by reducing overcrowding, traffic congestion, and pollution levels.

However, there are potential drawbacks to companies and businesses moving their premises outside metropolises. The main issue is that companies located in regional areas may be further away from their employees. This can make it more difficult to find labour to work in the company. As well as this, the companies may be located further away from their customers, which might weaken their relationships with their customers.

In conclusion, the merits to businesses relocating in more remote areas seem to outweigh the drawbacks as it can benefit the companies themselves, the local communities, and also the metropolitan areas. However, companies may face challenges to find labour and maintain close relationships with their customers. Given this situation it seems that the government should offer incentives to encourage companies to relocate to the countryside.

[256 words]

Notes:
1. With this particular type of opinion question (outweigh) it is safer to cover both sides of the argument.

2. As with other opinion essays you MUST clearly express your opinion about which side outweighs the other in the introduction and conclusion. In this case it is whether the advantages are greater than the disadvantages.

3. Note that the conclusion ends with a recommendation. More sample questions of opinion essays.

5.9. More sample questions of opinion essays

Some people believe that arts like museums and art galleries are not essential for a society and they should not be funded by the government.

What is your opinion?

More and more students choose to move to other countries to study their higher education.

Do you think the advantages of this outweigh its disadvantages?

Some people believe that local shopping markets are the best places to shop, while others believe that modern shopping centres are better.

Do the advantages of local markets outweigh the disadvantages?

To improve road safety there should be more severe punishments for drivers who break the rules.

To what extent do you agree or disagree?

It is believed that people who read a lot of novels have developed better imagination and language skills than people who prefer to watch TV.

To what extent do you agree or disagree?

There are many reasons that can motivate a person to stay working for the same company. Some believe that money is the main reason.

Do you agree or disagree?

Some believe that those who are not talented in language learning should not be required to learn a foreign language.

What is your opinion?

5.10. Common mistakes

Unclear opinion
In the example below the candidate fails to fully make clear their opinion in the introduction. The examiner can only guess that the candidate agrees, and has no idea of the extent. In this case this is not a good introduction, and this has a negative effect on task response and also cohesion and coherence.

> Television has brought great changes to the way many children spend their leisure time. Many people believe these changes have been beneficial.
>
> *To what extent do you agree or disagree?*

The candidate writes:

Nowadays, children spend a lot of time watching television. It seems that there are a wider variety of television shows and many more channels.

Choosing the wrong side to argue
For opinion essays I don't think you should think about what you really believe, you should think which side is easier to argue and use high-level language. In other words, the best side to choose is the one that you can maximize your score for the four grading criteria.

Contradicting your opinion
The example below shows how an opinion can easily be contradicted in the conclusion of an essay. The writer contradicts the opinion stated in the introduction that they somewhat disagree with the widespread use of technology, by stating in the conclusion that technology needs to be learnt.

> **Today, more and more young children have electronic gadgets such as computers and mobile phones. Some people say that this is a positive development. Do you agree or disagree?**

The candidate writes a contradicting opinion

In summary, <u>although it is necessary for children to learn to use these devices at a young age</u> I somewhat disagree that the widespread use of computers among children is a positive development.

Errors when making concessions

Essays that ask for your opinion have words in the question such as *"to what extent do you agree;"* "what is your opinion;" "do you agree or disagree." My advice to students is always to say that you totally agree/disagree and only focus on one side of the argument. I would only write "somewhat agree/disagree" if I didn't have enough things to say about one side of the argument. I have three main reasons for this.

First, it is more persuasive to totally agree/disagree and therefore leads to a higher score for task response. This is because when the examiner thinks about the extent you have convinced them of your opinion it is more powerful when you have just argued about one side.

The second reason is because it is much easier to structure an essay this way and it is easier to write it. In this case you are more likely to have fewer issues with cohesion and coherence and it will take less time to write the essay.

The third reason is because it is less likely you will end up arguing against yourself. I have read many essays where the writer says they "somewhat agree" but then they have gone on to write the body of the essay and less has been mentioned about agreeing than disagreeing. In this case, your score for task response will be limited to 6 because your opinion does not match the main points of your essay. As well as this your score for cohesion and coherence may be lowered because confusion may be created in the mind of the reader.

Finally, concessions (where you argue against your main position) can lead to total confusion when the candidate makes errors with grammar and vocabulary. In other words it is risky to write a concession because if you make errors with vocabulary and grammar the meaning can be totally unclear and then your score will go spiralling down for all four criteria.

6. Both sides and opinion essay

This type of essay tests your ability to discuss both sides of an argument and also give your own opinion and then support it with logical reasons. To score well you need to argue both sides of an argument clearly and give your own opinion along with a logical justification for it.

6.1. Typical question words

Discuss the advantages and disadvantages

Discuss the advantages and disadvantages and give your own opinion

Discuss both sides of this argument and then give your own opinion

Sample task

> Some people think that the education system should only focus on preparing students for employment, while others believe it has other important functions.
>
> *Discuss both sides and then give your own opinion.*

6.2. Task analysis

It is important to realise that every task contains a topic and a question. You must fully address both the topic and the question to score six and above for task response. An analysis of the topic and question is provided below:

Topic: Some people think that the education system should only focus on preparing students for employment, while others believe it has other important functions.

This type of topic always expresses two points of view. It is important to always see what the two points of view are. In this case the topic of the essay is about whether schools should only prepare students for their future careers or not. In other words it is **careers purposes vs. other purposes.**

Question: Discuss both sides and then give your own opinion.

The question has three requirements. You must discuss each side of the argument from a neutral point of view and then give your opinion, which is your view on the argument. In order to score a six and above you need to make sure you meet all three requirements of the question. To get to 7 you must answer all three requirements fully. In order to make your opinion clear I believe it is best to keep you opinion out of the introduction and body of the essay. If you put it into the introduction you risk making it sound like the essay is just about your opinion, which is misleading to the reader. If you put your opinion in the body of the essay, then you risk it becoming unclear to the examiner whether you have completed all three requirements. Essentially it becomes difficult to see both sides and your opinion. I believe it is best to hold your opinion for the conclusion of the essay. A typical error students make is to not say sufficient about their opinion. One sentence is clearly not enough to get to 7.

6.3. Planning your essay

1. **Underline key <u>vocabulary</u> in the topic and write words with the same or related meaning.**

   Some people think that the <u>education system</u> should only <u>focus on preparing</u> <u>students</u>

                         schools   *concentrate on*   *getting pupils ready*

   for <u>employment</u>, while others believe it has <u>other</u> <u>important functions</u>.

      career   *additional* *purposes*

2. **Decide what kind of response is needed.**

   Discuss both sides and then give your own opinion = you need to give reasons to support each side of the argument and then give your own personal opinion on the argument.

3. Brainstorm key points for the answer [two main points for each side of the argument is ideal]

Only preparing students for careers	Other functions
Leads to better careers and more $$$	Skills - to make the students well-rounded, such as communication skills and how to use technology
Leads to a better workforce which gives benefits to society	Morals and ethics - to make the society better

Your opinion
1. Both sides of the argument are merits
2. more strongly support **other functions**
...because if the students are well-rounded they will be more successful in their lives and contribute more to society

4. Decide on the structure of the essay

This essay is easy to structure for every question you can always structure it as follows:

Paragraph 1: Introduction

Paragraph 2: Side A of the argument [**Only preparing students for careers**]

Paragraph 3: Side B of the argument [**Other functions**]

Paragraph 4: Conclusion [**your opinion**]

6.4. Steps in writing your essay

Once you have written a solid plan for your essay, you can begin the task of actually writing the essay. Having a good plan will speed up this process and ensure that you meet all three requirements of this type of question [both sides and your opinion]. It will also ensure that you have a good balance for the essay. What I mean here is that you should cover both sides of the argument roughly equally. So, if you plan two points for each side of the argument this will help you to achieve it.

INTRODUCTION

1. Paraphrase the question

Given that you have already rephrased the keywords of the topic, in the planning stage, this step should be relatively easy. When you write this sentence, in addition to rephrasing words also try to rearrange the order of words in the sentence. This may necessitate changing some of the word forms. For instance you might have to change nouns into verbs. This shows the examiner your ability to use language flexibly and can increase your score for vocabulary and grammar.

> Some people think that the <u>education system</u> should only <u>focus on preparing students</u>
>
>   schools   concentrate on   getting pupils ready
>
> for <u>employment</u>, while others believe it has <u>other important functions</u>.
>
>   career   additional   purposes

Many people feel that getting pupils ready for their careers should be the main focus of schools, where as others believe that schools should have additional purposes.

2. Say what the essay is about

This sentence can always be written the same for every question of this type, as follows:

This essay discusses both sides of this argument, and then I will give my own perspective.

Nothing more is required in the introduction. You should try to memorise a sentence like this for this type of essay because you will be able to write it very quickly and without any errors with vocabulary and grammar. The introduction for this type of essay is the easiest of the three types of essays. If you want to use a slightly different sentence:

The purpose of this essay is to analyse both sides of this argument and then I will give my own perspective.

BODY

After you have written the introduction, you will need exactly two body paragraphs. You want a paragraph for each side of the argument. I suggest putting exactly two main points in each paragraph. A good paragraph should only have one main idea. The main idea of each paragraph is the side of the argument that it is focused on. After this you have two main points to support each side. You can then support each of these main points by explaining it or giving an example to illustrate it. In order to keep the size of your essay manageable, you might choose to have a major and minor point in each paragraph. The major point may use three sentences and the minor point 2 sentences. For instance, you might use this structure:

S1 topic sentence: make it clear which side of the argument you are discussing

s2: make the first main point

s3: explain the main point

s4: give an example to illustrate the main point

s5: make a second main point

s6: explain or give an example to illustrate the second main point

1. Write topic sentences for each body paragraph

Each body paragraph should start with a topic sentence. The topic sentence should make it clear to the reader which side of the argument the paragraph is about.

> *There are merits of schools only focusing on preparing young people for their working lives.*

2. Write supporting sentences for the topic sentences

You can think of the topic sentence you have just written as being the introduction for the paragraph. It introduces which side of the argument the paragraph is focusing on, which forms the key point for the paragraph. Having a clear key point for the paragraph makes it easy for the examiner to understand what you are saying in the paragraph. In addition, if the key point of the paragraph is clear any errors with vocabulary or grammar will be less likely to prevent communication. This is because the examiner will have more of a context to guess any parts that are unclear. After you have written the topic sentence, you should support it by developing the key point. There are three ways to develop your key point: Explanation, example, adding details

Explanation: *If young people are better prepared for their careers they will be more successful in their working lives.*

Adding details: *As well as this, they will also make more money and be able to support themselves better.*

Example: *To illustrate, some recent stories in the media highlighted that students who finish high school are less likely to be unemployed, and more likely to earn higher salaries.*

CONCLUSION

You should always signal the start of your concluding paragraph to the reader by using the words "*In conclusion*". Do not write "*to summarise*" or similar to begin this paragraph as you are not doing this; you are giving your own opinion. For this type of essay you should follow this with a phrase to make it clear that this final paragraph is about your opinion ....*I believe*. Generally your opinion can consist of three parts. The first part states that there are merits of both sides of the argument, which makes sense given that you have discussed these in the body of your essay. Second, you should give your opinion on the argument. The best way to do this is to say which side you support more strongly. Third, you should give a justification for your opinion. In other words you should state the reason why you more strongly support this side of the argument.

Essentially the structure is as follows:

1. Signal the start of your final paragraph.

2. State that both sides of the argument have merits.

3. Say which side you support more strongly.

4. Give a justification for supporting this side more strongly.

6.5. Model essay 1:

> Some people think that the education system should only focus on preparing students for employment, while others believe it has other important functions.
>
> *Discuss both sides and then give your own opinion.*

Many people feel that getting pupils ready for their careers should be the main focus of schools, where as others believe that schools should have additional purposes. This essay discusses both sides of this argument and then I will give my own perspective.

There are merits of schools only focusing on preparing young people for their working lives. If young people are better prepared for their careers they will be more successful in their working lives. As well as this, they will also make more money and be able to support themselves better. To illustrate, some recent stories in the media highlighted that students who finish high school are less likely to be unemployed, and more likely to earn higher salaries. In addition, by schools preparing young people for jobs there will be a better prepared workforce. This benefits society by raising productivity and ensuring that employers have the necessary labour they need.

However, there are also advantages of schools having other functions. First of all, they should teach students skills to make them well-rounded. By teaching communication skills and how to use technology the students will be better rounded individuals. Clearly, these are important skills in today's society and so they should be learnt at school. As well as this schools should teach morals and ethics because this will make the society better. Many people feel that this aspect of schooling has become neglected, and has led to a deterioration of society.

In conclusion, <u>I believe</u> both sides of the argument have their merits. On balance, however, it seems that schools should have other functions. This is because if the students are well-rounded they will be more successful in their lives and contribute more to society.

6.6. Template for a both sides and opinion essay

The template below contains about 130 words. The advantage of this template is that it can be used for any type of both sides and opinion essay. Memorising and using this template can help you to speed up the writing of your essay [you have less language to think of], and also help you to increase your score as you have a lower proportion of errors [this is error-free language], and also increase your score for vocabulary and grammar because the template has high-level vocabulary and grammar embedded in it..

INTRODUCTION

A highly controversial issue today relates to …………… In this essay, I am going to examine this question from both points of view and then give my own opinion on the matter.

BODY PARAGRAPH 1

On one side of the argument there are people who argue that the benefits of …………… considerably outweigh its disadvantages. The main reason for believing this is that ………………… It is also possible to say that ……. One good illustration of this is ………….

BODY PARAGRAPH 2

On the other hand, it is also possible to make the opposing case. It is often argued that in fact ………… People often have this opinion because …………… A second point is that ………..A particularly good example here is…………..

CONCLUSION

In conclusion, I believe both arguments have their merits. On balance, however, I feel that… This is because….

6.7. Model essay 2: *[based on the template on the previous page]*

> **Some people believe that there should be the death penalty for extremely serious crimes. Others believe that it is not morally correct to kill criminals.**
>
> *Discuss both these views and give your own opinion.*

A highly controversial issue today relates to capital punishment. In this essay, I am going to examine this question from both points of view and then give my own opinion on the matter.

On one side of the argument there are people who argue that the benefits of killing violent criminals considerably outweigh its disadvantages. The main reason for believing this is that the fear of execution acts as a deterrent to commit serious crimes such as rape and murder. It is also possible to say that the execution of a criminal may bring relief to the suffering victims. One good illustration of this is when Saddam Hussein was executed. Many of the victims who were persecuted under his rule expressed joy and relief when he was finally captured and killed.

On the other hand, it is also possible to make the opposing case. It is often argued that in fact sentencing criminals to death is just committing another murder. People often have this opinion because they think that it is immoral to take another person's life, no matter what the reason is. A second point is that many religions are opposed to any form of murder. A particularly good example here is from the bible, which lists killing another person as one of the Ten Commandments that should not be broken.

In conclusion, I believe both arguments have their merits. On balance, however, I feel that capital punishment is justified. This is because in cases of extreme crime and that deterring crime is more important than taking the moral high ground.   [267 words]

6.8. More Sample Questions

There are two main types of questions here. The first kind requires you to discuss the advantages and disadvantages of one thing and the second kind asks you to discuss the advantages of two different things.

Situation one: discuss the advantages and disadvantages of one thing.

Computers are being used more and more in education. Discuss the advantages and disadvantages of computers and then give your opinion.

The structure is:

Introduction

advantages of computers

disadvantages of computers

your opinion

Situation two: discuss the advantages of two different things

Some people say that learning online is the best way to learn, whereas some claim that it is still better to attend a class with a teacher. Discuss both sides of this argument and then give your opinion

The structure is:

Introduction

advantages of online learning

advantages of teachers

your opinion

More sample tasks for both sides and opinion essays

These days, many people live or work overseas in a different country than they were born in.

Discuss the advantages and disadvantages of this and then give your own opinion.

Technology allows food to be produced in greater quantities and at lower prices. Some people believe this is a positive development, while others feel that the change is harmful.

Discuss both views and give your own opinion.

It is more important to spend public money on promoting a healthy lifestyle, in order to prevent illness rather than to spend it on the treatment of people who are already ill.

Discuss the advantages and disadvantages of this and then give your own opinion.

Some people think that development in technology causes environmental problems. Other people believe that technology can solve environmental problems.

Discuss both sides of the argument and then give your opinion.

Some people believe that to improve public health more public sports facilities should be provided by the government; others believe that this will have little effect and other measures are needed to improve people's health.

Discuss both sides of the argument and then give your opinion.

Some people think computers and the Internet are important in children's study, but others think students are usually distracted by these and they should not be used during class time.

Discuss both sides of this argument and give your own opinion.

6.9. Common mistakes

Putting your opinion in the introduction of the essay

For this type of essay it is best to keep your opinion for the final paragraph. Writing this here makes it seem like this essay is just about your opinion. Instead you should write: "*This essay discusses both sides of this argument and then I will give my own perspective.*"

> Some people think that spending a lot on holding wedding parties, birthday parties and other celebrations is just a waste of money. Others, however, think that these are necessary for individuals and the society.
>
> *Discuss both views and give your opinion.*

The candidate writes a misleading introduction below:

Today, holding parties or other activities is a common practice for individuals and organisations to celebrate some special events. Some people, however, claim that these celebrations are wasteful, while others argue that they have favourable effects on individuals and the society. <u>Personally, I believe that holding these celebrations does more good than harm.</u>

Putting your opinion in the body of the essay

The question asks for both views and your opinion. Try to have three clear responses. Hold your opinion until the final paragraph. It is extremely dangerous to mix your opinion with one of the sides because some examiners will then feel you have not satisfactorily completed the task of both sides and your opinion. They might think you have only discussed one side and your opinion. It's very risky to mix your opinion with the discussion of one side of the argument. Taking this risk may mean you will not get to 7 for task response; it will depend on the examiner's interpretation. To get rid of this risk I suggest you structure the essay the way I have outlined, with your opinion given in the final paragraph only. You can see the previous model essay in this section for examples of this.

Not writing enough for your opinion

With a both sides and opinion essay, your opinion is one of the three requirements of the task. You must give more than a sentence for your opinion. In addition, you should not only say what your opinion is but also give the reason. You can see the previous model essay in this section for examples of this. I suggest you say the following:

1. Start with a signal "In conclusion, I believe..."

2. State that both sides of the argument are important/have merits

3. State which one is more important/better

4. Say why. Justify your selection. This is the key to reaching 7 and above for task response. Remember that YOUR opinion is one of the three parts of the question and although this paragraph may be briefer than the body paragraphs it is a very important one.

7. Two question essay

This type of question sometimes also known as a *problem and solution essay*. I do not call it this because it is not always about *problems* and *solutions*. This type of question tests your ability to discuss two aspects of an issue. To score well you must answer BOTH questions well. Therefore you should respond to each of the questions equally.

7.1. *Sample question words*

What problem does this cause?

What are some potential solutions?

What are the causes of this problem?

What are some potential solutions?

Do you agree or disagree?

What are some solutions?

Sample task

> Some people think that in the future lots of changes will occur that will improve our society.
> *Do you agree or disagree?*
> *What kind of changes will occur?*

7.2. *Task analysis*

It is important to realise that every task contains a topic and a question. You must fully address both the topic and the question to score six and above for task response. An analysis of the topic and question is provided below:

Topic: Some people think that in the future lots of changes will occur that will improve our society.

Question 1: *Do you agree or disagree?*

Question 2: *What kind of changes will occur?*

7.3. Planning the essay

1. **Underline key <u>vocabulary</u> in the topic and write words with the same or related meaning.**

   Some people think that in the <u>future</u> lots of <u>changes will occur</u> that will

   in the years to come   developments are going to happen

   <u>improve</u> our <u>society</u>.

   make life better

2. **Decide what kind of response is needed.**

   Do you agree or disagree? = *Say whether you agree or disagree*

   What kind of changes will occur? = *State what changes might happen*

3. **Brainstorm key points for the answer.**

Question one: agree the changes will be positive	Question two: changes that will occur
Life is becoming more convenient [technology leads to convenience]	More time-saving technology, such as robots to do our housework.
Better entertainment	New technologies to enhance our entertainment. For instance 3-D television will soon become commonplace in our living rooms.

4. Decide on the structure of the essay

This essay can always be structured the same based on the two questions that are asked:

introduction = rephrase the topic and introduce both questions

question one = write exactly two main points to support your response

question two = write exactly two main points to support your response

conclusion = summarise your main points about each question

7.4. Steps in writing your essay

Once you have written a solid plan for your essay, you can begin the task of actually writing the essay. Having a good plan will speed up this process and ensure that you are consistent with your opinion throughout the essay. What I mean here is that the introduction will fit the body of the essay, and the conclusion will summarise the points from the body of the essay. If you achieve this high level of fit, you are likely to score well for task response and cohesion and coherence.

INTRODUCTION

1. Paraphrase the question

Given that you have already rephrased the keywords of the topic this step should be relatively easy. When you do write this sentence, in addition to rephrasing words also try to rearrange the order of words in the sentence. This may necessitate changing some of the word forms. For instance you might have to change nouns into verbs. This shows the examiner your ability to use language flexibly and can increase your score for vocabulary and grammar.

Some people think that in the <u>future</u> lots of <u>changes will occur</u> that will

in the years to come   *developments are taking place*

<u>improve</u> our <u>society</u>.

make life better

As a result of developments that are taking place, many people believe that life will become better.

2. Introduce what the essay is about

It is important to make it clear what the essay is about because it makes it clear to the examiner you understand that there are two questions. Also, when the examiner reads the body of your essay they already have an overall idea of what your essay is about, and in the likely event that you have errors with vocabulary and grammar they may be less serious because the examiner will have more of a context in order to guess the meaning of what you are trying to express. You can simply state what the essay is about using a phrase like:

This essay discusses,

...and then add on a rephrase of the two questions:

This essay discusses the reasons why the changes that are coming are positive, and also suggests what kind of changes will occur.

BODY

After you have written the introduction, you will need exactly two body paragraphs. You should have a paragraph for each of the questions. A good paragraph should only have one main idea. The main idea for each paragraph is the question you are responding to. You should then have exactly two main points to support each question. This ensures that you get the right balance for the essay. What I mean here is that you should say about the same amount for each of the questions. You should not focus on one of the questions more than the other. You can then support each of these main points by explaining it or giving an example to illustrate it. In order to keep the size of your essay manageable, you might choose to have a major and minor point in each paragraph. The major point may use three sentences and the minor point 2 sentences. For instance, you might use this structure:

s1 topic sentence: make it clear which question you are discussing

s2: introduce the main point

s3: explain the main point

s4: give an example to illustrate the main point

s5: minor point

s6: explain or give an example to illustrate the minor point

1. Write topic sentences for each body paragraph

Each body paragraph should start with a topic sentence. For this type of essay the topic sentence should clearly identify which of the questions is being responded to.

The changes that are coming are positive for two main reasons

[Responds to causes]

2. Write supporting sentences for the topic sentences

You can think of the topic sentence you have just written as being the introduction for the paragraph. It introduces the question you are responding to, which forms the key point for the paragraph. Having a clear key point for the paragraph makes it easy for the examiner to understand what you are saying in the paragraph. In addition, if the key point of the paragraph is clear any errors with vocabulary or grammar will be less likely to prevent communication. This is because the examiner will have more of a context to guess any parts that are unclear. After you have written the topic sentence, you should support it by developing the key point. There are three ways to develop your key point: Explanation, example, adding details

Explanation: *The main reason is that they will make our lives more convenient.*

Adding details: *We are likely to have more free time as a result of technology taking over many of our everyday tasks.*

Example: *For example, we may have robots capable of doing many household chores.*

CONCLUSION

You only need to do two things in the final paragraph of this type of essay and they are always the same. First you need to signal that this is the concluding paragraph and second you should summarise your main points for each question.

In conclusion, the future looks promising because we will have technology takeover many of life's mundane tasks and we'll have better forms of entertainment. The most likely changes appeared to be technologies to save us time and also enhance our leisure time.

7.5. Model essay one:

> Some people think that in the future lots of changes will occur that will improve our society.
>
> Do you agree or disagree?
>
> What kind of changes will occur?

As a result of developments that are taking place, many people believe that life will become better. This essay discusses the reasons why the changes that are coming are positive, and also suggests what kind of changes will occur.

The changes that are coming are positive for two main reasons. The main reason is that they will make our lives more convenient. We are likely to have more free time as a result of technology taking over many of our everyday tasks. For example, we may have robots capable of doing many household chores, and this will enable us to have more free time for enjoyment and relaxation. Another factor is that our recreational time will be enhanced by new technologies that make our entertainment and even more fun. If we enjoy ourselves more we will be happier and more relaxed.

There are two main types of developments that are likely to occur. The first of these is time-saving technologies. Future enhancements of robotics are likely to lead to even more household tasks being performed by machines. As well as this, the entertainment industry looks likely to soon make enhancements to our recreational experiences by making new technologies available. A good example of this is 3-D television, which will make watching movies even more fun.

In conclusion, the future looks promising because we will have technology takeover many of life's mundane tasks and we'll have better forms of entertainment. The most likely changes appear to be technologies to save us time and also enhance our leisure time.

[256 words]

7.6. Template for a two question essay

It is difficult to build a standardised template for our two question essay because a wide variety of questions can be asked. First a general template will be given and then a more specific template will be given for a typical problem and solution essay.

General template

Introduction

Rephrase the topic

this essay discusses...[Question one] + [question two]

Body

Question one [try to write two main points to respond to this question]

Question two [try to write two main points to respond to this question]

Conclusion

In conclusion,
[summarise the two main points about question one]
[summarise the two main points about question two]

Template for the problem and solution essay that follows with gaps for the topic
Note that this is the original form of a two question essay that gets asked and it is essentially the same as the essay above and follows the same format. The question type is quite commonplace and you can use the template below for any essay of this type.

………… *is becoming increasingly serious in many nations. Although ………… Threaten[s] many societies, its /their effects can also be combated successfully. This essay looks at some of the problems caused by ………… on society, and suggests some solutions to the problems.*

………… *causes multiple problems. The ………… effects are very obvious. For example, ………… In some cases, such as ………… even leads to (death). The second effect is ………… People who ………… become …………*

However, the menace of ………… can be fought. Education is the main way to tackle this issue. People need to be aware of the effects so that they can avoid this problem. In addition, the government could also ………… This is a good approach because …………

In conclusion, ………… is a serious issue because it causes harmful effects on people's health and people who are ………… The best approaches to deal with it are to educate people about its damaging effects, and also for the government to ………… Although the problem is unlikely to be entirely eliminated in the short term there are concrete steps to reduce the effects it is having on the current society.

[about 175 words]

7.7. Model essay two:
[problem and solution]

> The use of illegal drugs, such as heroin and cocaine, are becoming more and more common in many countries.
>
> What are some of the problems associated with drug abuse, and what are some of the possible solutions?

Change the underlined parts according to your topic

Drug abuse is becoming increasingly serious in many nations. Although drugs threaten many societies, their effects can also be combated successfully. This essay looks at some of the problems caused by drug use on society, and suggests some solutions to the problems.

Drug abuse causes multiple problems for countries and communities. The medical effects are very obvious. For example, addicts abuse their bodies and neglect their health, and so eventually require expensive treatment or hospitalization. In some cases, such as Marilyn Monroe, a drug overdose even leads to death. The second effect is crime. People who take drugs become crazy and irrational and often cause harm and danger to themselves and others.

However, the menace of drugs can be fought. Education is the main way to tackle this issue. People need to be aware of the effects so that they can avoid this problem. In addition, the government could also use infomercials to educate their citizens. This is a good approach because they can alert all citizens about the negative aspects of using drugs.

In conclusion, drug abuse is a serious issue because it causes harmful effects on people's health and people who are high often commit crimes. The best approaches to deal with it are to educate people about its damaging effects, and also for the government to ensure all people are aware of the consequences through public service advertising. Although the problem is unlikely to be entirely eliminated in the short term these are concrete steps to reduce the effects it is having on the current society.

[260 words]

7.8. More sample questions

Nowadays we communicate less with our family members face to face.
What are the causes of this?
What are some potential solutions?

More people use their own cars rather than public transport; so many people believe it is up to the government to encourage people to use public transport.
Do you agree?
How else can people be encouraged to use public transportation?

The development of technology has influenced the ways people interact with each other.
What are the main changes in the types of interactions people have?
Do you think this is positive or negative?

Developed countries often give financial aid to developing countries, but it does not solve poverty, so developed countries should give other types of help to the poor countries rather than financial aid.
Do you agree or disagree?
What other kind of aid could be provided?

There are many reasons that can motivate a person to stay working for the same company. Some believe that money is the main reason.
Do you agree or disagree?
What are some other reasons why people may stay?

7.9. Common mistakes

Not responding fully to both questions

Level 6 for task response requires that you: *Address all parts of the task although some parts may be more fully covered than others.* Level 7 requires that you: *Fully address all parts of the task.* From this perspective it is vital that you answer both questions fully in order to reach 7 and above.

Not introducing BOTH questions in the introduction.

As mentioned above it is vital that your essay focuses on both questions in the essay. It is misleading to only introduce one of the questions in the introduction.

8. Improving your score

This section will help you to improve your score by outlining some of the common errors that occur with essays written in the exam and also to make suggestion about how to enhance your score for each of the four grading criteria.

8.1. Common mistakes with task response

From my experience working as an IELTS examiner, IELTS tutor, and also as an online editor of thousands of IELTS essays I have discovered that students make the following mistakes on their essays.

Poor time management

If you do not right enough words your score for task response is penalised by 1 to 3 points! In addition to that, if you didn't complete the task you are unlikely to score well for task response anyway, as you are unlikely to have completely answered the question. In this case your score for task response would be restricted to 5 and you would still get the penalty on top of this. In other words you probably will fail your exam! The following are my suggestions for managing your time:

Make sure you make a plan before you start writing. A plan will save you time when you start writing because you will not have to keep stopping to think about what point you want to make next. This is the area that most students do poorly on and in order to do it well it takes practice. The best way to practice is to look at past exam questions and prepare a plan of how you would write them.

Make sure you have practiced writing sufficiently before your exam and that you understand how to structure the three types of essays that get asked. If you are familiar with the types of questions that get asked you won't get a nasty surprise and you will be able to answer the question more quickly.

If you really have trouble with finishing on time, learn some stock phrases that you can write quickly in the exam. If you have learnt the sentences well you will be able to write them quickly and without errors. The best way to learn these is to look at model answers and underline sentences you think you would like to use in your own writing. Then you need to memorize the sentences by writing them, and even better, practice writing them in an essay.

Not responding to all parts of the topic.

For the task below, the topic includes two parts that must be both referred to in the body of the essay. These two parts are <u>cheaper</u> and <u>easier</u>. If you have failed to answer both, your score would be limited to 5 for task response.

These days, due to advances in technology, it is <u>cheaper</u> and <u>easier</u> to travel abroad.

Do the advantages outweigh the disadvantages?

Misstating the topic

This error occurs when a candidate gives an answer that is not directly related to the topic; or in other words, is tangential to the topic. This commonly occurs in the introduction to the essay but also it can happen in the body of the essay. See the example below, the question talks about space travel but the candidate talks about science and technology in general.

> Some people think space travel is important for the development of humanity; while other people believe it is a waste of money. Discuss both views and give your opinion.

<u>Candidate writes:</u>

Many people believe that we should invest more money on science. However, others disagree and think we should not waste money on technology. This essay discusses both sides of the argument and then I will give my opinion.

In the example below the candidate changes the topic by saying that people *rely on computers* instead of talking about whether they will be able to use *computers to view art*.

> Some people claim that public museums and art galleries will not be needed because people can see historical objects and works of art by using a computer. Do you agree or disagree with this opinion?

<u>Candidate writes:</u>

Nowadays, people tend to <u>rely on computers</u> too much. Some people even think the need for public museums and art galleries will gradually disappear in the future. I totally disagree because I believe museums and galleries will always be essential.

In the example below the candidate changes the topic by rephrasing power of advertising to deceptive advertising. The task does not say that advertising is deceptive only that it is powerful.

> Today, the high sales of popular consumer goods reflect the <u>power of advertising</u> and not the real needs of the society in which they are sold.
>
> To what extent do you agree or disagree?

Candidate writes:

These days, we can see some consumer goods are in high demand in our society. There exists a perception that such high demand is the result of <u>deceptive advertising</u>. I somewhat agree with this.

The question says <u>more</u> not <u>only</u>

> **Some people said the government should not spend money on building theaters and sports stadiums. It should spend more money on medical care and education. Do you agree or disagree?**

Candidate writes:

When it comes to how to allocate the governmental budget, one topic now under debate is whether the money should be <u>spent only</u> on medical services and education instead of on constructing theaters and sports stadiums.

Not fully answering the question

For the question below note that you need to not only mention the advantages and disadvantages but also state which one is stronger. A common error is to just state the advantages and disadvantages. The problem here is that the candidate appears to be focusing on the advantages and disadvantages and not on which one outweighs the other, as required by the question.

> Some museums and art galleries charge admission fees, while others have free entry.
> Do you think the advantages of free admission <u>outweigh</u> the disadvantages?

Candidate writes:

Some museums and art galleries are free, whereas others require payment for entry. This essay discusses the advantages and disadvantages.

Misstating the question

In the example below the candidate makes it seem like the question is only asking for their opinion instead of both sides of the argument and their own opinion.

> Technology allows food to be produced in greater quantities and at lower prices. Some people believe this is a positive development, while others feel that the change is harmful.
> *Discuss both views and give your own opinion.*

The candidate writes:

Nowadays our food supply is more plentiful and cheaper due to scientific advances. <u>I believe</u> this is totally advantageous for individuals and society for the reasons that follow.

Over-generalisation

Overgeneralisation occurs when something is exaggerated. Something that only applies to some or the majority is said to apply to all of a population.

For example: *As we all know, <u>all</u> politicians are corrupt.*

8.2. Improving task response

Read the task carefully

Do not rush reading the task, even though you are under pressure to finish the writing exam in one hour. Read every word carefully and underline key words. Think carefully what the topic is about and what the question is asking you to say about the topic.

Planning

The planning stage should also not be rushed. You should spend at least 5 minutes planning your essay. You need to make sure that you have strong main ideas and a good structure for your essay. This will enable you to focus on the topic and question. Also, if you make an effective plan, this can actually speed up the writing of your essay. This is because a lot of time can be wasted when writing if you need to think of what you are going to say. The plan can reduce the time spent trying to think of what to say when writing. Essentially, it's more time efficient to do all the thinking at the start, in the planning stage, in order to reduce the time spent thinking during writing.

Developing strong main ideas

A lot of my students tell me they struggle to come up with good ideas. My main suggestion is to practice this. Look at lots of sample questions and think how you would answer them. You may get lucky and get one of these questions in your exam! As well as this, brainstorming in English is a skill and if you practice it you will get better at it.

Developing your ideas well

A grade six requires responding to all parts of the question. A grade seven and above requires that you extend and support your ideas. This can be done by supporting your main ideas with explanations, details, and examples. For more on this see the section on writing the body of the essay.

Use an appropriate structure

To get a high score it is essential that you structure your ideas well. This is because the examiner will be able to see the quality of your ideas if they are structured well.

8.3. Common errors with cohesion and coherence

Avoid basic sequencing words

Try to avoid sample sequencing words such as: *firstly secondly*, as they are very basic sequences. Instead use something like: *the main reason….another factor*

> ~~Firstly~~, <u>The main benefit is that</u> students can get access to resources online with their computers anytime they want. This is of benefit for those who are not able to attend class at a certain time. ~~Secondly~~, <u>As well as this</u>, students can choose where to study, and this is clearly a benefit to students who need to look after other members of their family.

Avoid unnecessary sentence elements

In the examples below unnecessary phrases are underlined. It is better to leave these out because they don't add anything to the sentence, and they break the flow of the sentence. In other words, they lower coherence, while offering no communicative benefit.

There are, <u>to tell the truth</u>, tutors and doctors in every city even in the countryside.

In my opinion, <u>however</u>, doctors are still important.

Incorrect use of conjunctions

Words like: *however, consequently, in addition* can be used to start sentences. When you use a conjunction it is to join two parts of a sentence and you should only have a single sentence. Words that cannot be used to start sentences and should only be used in the middle of sentences are called conjunctions. You can remember them as FANBOYS:

For: He is betting with his health, <u>for</u> he has been smoking far too long.

And: They bet <u>and</u> they drink.

Nor: They do not bet <u>nor</u> do they drink.

But: They bet, <u>but</u> they don't drink.

Or: Every day they bet <u>or</u> they drink.

Yet: They bet, <u>yet</u> they don't drink.

So: He bet well last night, <u>so</u> he drank a beer to celebrate.

Not using an appropriate structure for the question type

In response to the question below, a student wrote: *I discussed both views and end up getting 6 bands. Really disappointed.*

My reply: that's because you were not asked to discuss both views. You were asked to discuss which one is better!

> More houses are needed in many countries to cope with increasing populations. Would it be <u>better</u> to build houses in existing towns and cities or to develop new towns in rural areas?

Avoid irrelevant sentences

Every supporting sentence in a paragraph must relate to the main idea stated in the topic sentence. A sentence that does not support the main idea does not belong in the paragraph, thus such a sentence should be omitted. When a sentence does not belong in a paragraph, it is called an irrelevant sentence. The underlined sentence below is an example of this because it is not about where people come from, like the rest of the paragraph:

The staff in the company come from many different parts of the world. Some are from European countries, such as France, Spain, and Italy. Others are from Middle Eastern countries like Saudi Arabia and Israel. Still other students were born in Asian countries, including Japan and Korea. Japanese food is delicious. The largest number of employees are from Latin American countries like Mexico, Venezuela and Peru. The company is an interesting mix of people from many different countries.

8.4. Improving cohesion and coherence

Make a plan before you start writing

If you have a solid plan before you start writing you will make sure that you are on topic and that you have an appropriate structure for your essay. It is essential that you respond to the question that is asked.

Use sequencing words and connecting phrases

Sequencing words and connecting phrases add cohesion to your writing by showing the relationship between ideas and by sending signals to the reader about your writing. To improve this, refer to Section 10: Useful Linking Words and Phrases.

Avoid errors with word choices

If you make lots of errors with word choices this makes it more difficult for the examiner to read your writing which lowers coherence. Therefore these errors with word choices lower your score for vocabulary as well as for cohesion and coherence. The negative effect is double!

Avoid unnecessarily complicated structures and grammar

The more difficult it is for the examiner to follow your writing the lower your score for cohesion and coherence. Just use simple straightforward main points and explain them as clearly and logically as possible. In terms of sentence structure avoid sentences with lots of clauses. I would say a maximum of three clauses. This is because sentences with lots of clauses are hard to read and also if you make any errors with vocabulary or grammar the reader will become totally confused.

Learn how to develop your ideas in paragraphs

When assessing your score for cohesion and coherence the examiner is looking at your ability to structure the whole essay and also your ability to structure individual paragraphs. Paragraphs should focus on one main idea and then that idea should be logically developed in the paragraph through explanation, adding details, and using examples that illustrate the main point. For a more detailed explanation of this refer to section 4.2 on the body of the essay.

8.5. Common errors with vocabulary

"S" endings of words

Almost every essay I read has this mistake. The writer puts an "S" where it's not needed or else forgets to put one where it is needed. Examples below:

Student ~~are~~ always studying hard. ["s" is needed for students]

Students ~~goes~~ home tired every day. [The verb should be *go*]

Technologies ~~are~~ developing rapidly. [Technology is uncountable in this context so it should be technology *is* developing rapidly]

Other errors with word endings and form

Other common errors are errors with word endings such as "ed" for past tense, and errors with word forms such as when a verb is incorrectly written as a noun. A couple of examples:

Last year my uncle ~~work~~ in America. [worked]

We need to ~~management~~ the environment better. [manage]

Repeating words excessively

You should always rephrase words that are given in the task because it shows your ability to rephrase words and that you have a broad vocabulary. In addition to this, try to avoid repeating the same word in the body of your essay. You can achieve this by using different words or by using different forms of the same word.

Example of rephrase: *country = nation*

Example of change in form: *young people need to be prepared for their careers = preparation of young people for their careers is necessary*

Noun trains [where you have a whole lot of nouns together; like cars on the train].

This error occurs when two or more nouns are together, it would be more natural to write "application of pesticides" than" pesticides application" you can Google both of these [using speech marks] and see that "application of pesticides" is much more common and the results fit your context better. If you are ever unsure whether one phrase is better than another, whether two words go together, or about the word order of a sentence you can use this method of googling the phrases. Some other examples:

starvation alleviation = alleviation of starvation

food production revolution = revolutionising food production

Obvious memorised language that is inappropriately applied

Below are examples of obvious memorised phrases that are incorrectly applied.

One of the most controversial issues relates to whether students should live at home or on campus.

My response: Really! I wasn't aware. I thought was things like abortion and euthanasia and wars! Better to say "A highly debated issue"

Whether children should start learning a foreign language at primary school instead of high school has sparked off an intensive debate.

My response: Really! I wasn't aware. I have heard nothing about this. Better to say "... is an important issue in the field of education"

Colloquial expressions

Some phrases are used when speaking, but not when writing. Some examples:

actually, I would also like to mention, I reckon

Clichés

A cliché is an overused expression. These can be considered as "ugly" English. Examples:

In this day and age...

At the end of the day...

Just like every coin has two sides...

8.6. Improving vocabulary

This is such a huge area that it is beyond the scope of this book. However, some general guidelines follow. You can also see some words and phrases for common topics in Section 9: Vocabulary for Common Topics. Also, you can view my website:
http://www.ieltsanswers.com/IELTS-Vocabulary.html

Rephrase the task

The first thing you should do when you start the writing exam is read the question and underline key words. This is to help you clearly understand the question and also to help you generate some alternative words to replace the given words. This shows the examiner your ability to rephrase and also that you have a broad vocabulary.

Use high-level words where possible

Where possible try to avoid basic words and use high-level words to show the examiner your talent with language. Do not forget that it is a language test! If you want to improve your vocabulary you can refer here: http://www.ieltsanswers.com/IELTS-Vocabulary.html

8.7. Common errors with grammar

Articles

Almost every essay I read has errors with articles. The articles are: a, an, the

To reduce these errors you should read about the rules, do some quizzes, and also practice your writing and get feedback on these. More is explained about this in the next section on improving grammar.

Avoid writing short simple sentences

In order to score six and above you need to show the examiner you have the ability to write complex sentences. These are sentences that have a dependent and independent clause. If you just write short simple sentences like the one below your score is limited to 5.

The advantages of this policy are obvious. It is beneficial for communities and societies in general.

My comment: It would be better to write this as one sentence: "The advantages of this policy for communities and societies are obvious. "

He or she

If you write in plural you don't need to use the awkward expression "he *or she*. Write "*if people like it... they*"; instead of: "*if a person likes it he or she...*"

8.8. Improving grammar

Grammar is a huge area with tons of books dedicated to it. If you are taking an IELTS exam in the near future you may not have a lot of time to work on grammar. The best ways to improve your grammar score are to reduce the number of errors you make and also to write a variety of sentence types. Looking below at the grading criteria for a level 7 for grammar makes this clear.

Criteria for grammar

- uses a variety of complex structures
- produces frequent error-free sentences
- has good control of grammar and punctuation but may make a few errors

From the criteria above we can notice that there is nothing about using complicated tenses such as perfect tenses. Spending time on learning different tenses and how to use them does not usually pay off well in terms of the time investment. As well is this, they are difficult to master and apply in your writing. For this reason I think that it's better to focus on reducing errors and learning to write different sentence structures, especially complex sentences. This section focuses on some ways to write complex sentence structures and then on explaining a few of the types of grammatical errors that commonly occur in essays.

Develop ways of writing complex sentences

Complex sentences are sentences that include an independent and dependent clause. Two excellent ways to form these are to use conditionals [phrases] and relative clauses [who, which, that, where]. To read about the rules and do some quizzes go here:

http://www.ieltsanswers.com/IELTS-Grammar.html

Conditional sentences

A conditional sentence is a complex sentence structure used to talk about something that occurs only if something else happens. The condition may be something real or imagined, and the result could be a definite result, or just a possible result. Conditionals are a useful way of forming complex sentences, which can boost your grammar score. Another reason why I teach candidates to use them is because they can be easily noticed by an examiner, due to the word *if*. If sends a signal to the examiner that a conditional is being used.

There are two clauses to a conditional sentence:

One part is the **if** clause. This is the event that needs to occur. It is a dependent clause because it is not a complete sentence and is dependent on the other part of the sentence.

The second part is the **result** or main clause, or what happens when the event in the **if** clause occurs. The result clause is an independent clause because it can stand on its own as a sentence.

The dependent and independent clauses can be written in any order, as shown below:

If I have holidays, I go to Australia. [A comma as needed when the dependent clause comes first]

I go to Australia if I have holidays. [No comma]

Summary of conditions

Condition	Usage	Example
0	Facts and opinions	If I have holidays, I go to Australia present tense, present tense
1	Likely outcomes	If I have enough days off, I will go to Australia. Present tense future tense
2	Unlikely outcomes or imagined situations	If I won the lottery, I would go to Australia. Past tense would
3	Past situations that didn't occur	If I had had enough days off, I would have gone to Australia. Past Perfect Tense would have

Note: To read more about the rules about conditionals and do some quizzes go here: http://www.ieltsanswers.com/IELTS-Grammar.html

Relative clauses

Another good way to increase your grammar score by using complex sentences, is to add relative clauses to your sentences. Relative clauses use relative pronouns (that, which, who,) and are dependent clauses, which means that they cannot stand on their own as complete sentence.

Summary of relative pronouns

Relative pronoun	Use	Example
who	people	I like students who study hard.
which	things	I live in a flat, which is in a high-rise building.
where	places	I like shopping at places where there is lots of parking.
whose	possession	Do you know the boy whose mother is a nurse?
that	for a specific person or thing	I don't like the table that stands in the kitchen.

Note: To read more about the rules about relative clauses and do some quizzes go here: http://www.ieltsanswers.com/IELTS-Grammar.html

8.9. Reduce errors

The second way to increase your score is to reduce errors. To get to grade 7 and above you need to have frequent error-free sentences. If you do not have this you cannot get to 7 and above. If you want to get to 8 or 9 you need to decrease errors to a similar frequency as a native writer. In order to achieve this you need to identify your areas of weakness and work on these by learning the rules, doing quizzes, and getting feedback on your writing. If you want me to assess your writing refer here:

http://www.ieltsanswers.com/IELTS-Writing-Correction.html

Articles (A, An, the)

An article is a word that is used with a noun to indicate to the reader whether the noun is a particular and specific noun or an instance of a noun in general., There are two types of articles the indefinite (a/an), which refers to the general usage of a noun; and the definite article (the) which refers to a specific noun that will be identifiable by the reader.

An **indefinite** article indicates that its noun is not a specific one that can be identified by the reader. It may be something that the writer is mentioning for the first time, or the writer may be making a general statement about something. The indefinite articles are *a* and *an*. The word *a is used* before words that begin with a consonant sound (even if the word starts with a vowel, as in *a unicorn*). *An* is used before words that begin with a vowel sound (even if the word starts with a consonant, as in *an hour*).

Example: *She had **a** house so large that **an** elephant would get lost.*

A **definite** article is used with a noun that refers to something specific the reader should be aware of. It may be used to refer back to something that the speaker has already mentioned, or it may be used with a noun that has only one possible instance [*The capital of China is Beijing*]. The definite article, *the,* can be used for both singular and plural nouns.

Example: *The best place to live is the capital.*

Summary of the usage of articles

	Indefinite (*a* or *an*)	**Definite** (*the*)
Singular	a cat (any cat) an orange (any orange)	the dirtiest cat the red orange
	[None used]	**Definite** (*the*)
Plural	Plurals, languages, sports, subjects, cities, countries… with a few exceptions!	The best cats) the sweetest oranges

Note the following:

1. First versus subsequent mention of a noun

A or an is used to introduce a noun when it is used for the first time in a piece of writing.

"Please give me a pen."

The is used afterward each time you mention that same noun.

"Where is the pen?"

There was a cat in my room. When my dog came in, the cat ran away.

2. Zero articles:

Some common types of nouns that don't take an article are:

a. Plurals usually have no articles: "please give me some apples," "I like apples.;" unless they are definite "these are the best apples.

b. Names of languages and nationalities: "I am Chinese."

c. Names of sports: "I like playing soccer."

d. Names of academic subjects: "I studied math for three years."

3. Places usually have no article:

Do not use *the* before names of streets, countries, lakes, and mountains.

There are a few exceptions such as: the USA, the UK, the EU [note that these are all areas that are made up of different regions]; likewise with groups of lakes like the Great Lakes, and ranges of mountains like the Himalayas.

Note: To read more about the rules about articles and do some quizzes go here: http://www.ieltsanswers.com/IELTS-Grammar.html

Prepositions

Prepositions are used to locate something in time and space, modify a noun; or tell when or where or under what conditions something happened. The following are guidelines for using prepositions correctly. This covers many common situations. However, you need to refer to my website or other sources for an exhaustive list: http://www.ieltsanswers.com/IELTS-Grammar.html

Prepositions of Time: at, in, on

Preposition	Usage	Example
At	*at* is for specific times	The exam is <u>at</u> 12:15 PM
In	*in* is for nonspecific times during a day/month/year.	The exam is <u>in</u> the morning
On	*on* for days and dates	The exam is <u>on</u> Monday. The exam is <u>on</u> Christmas Day.

Prepositions of Place: at, in, on

Preposition	Usage	Example
At	We use **at** for specific addresses.	I live at 50 Pong Lai Road.
In	We use **in** for the names of land-areas (towns, counties, states, countries, and continents).	I live in Taipei.
On	We use **on** for the names of streets, avenues, etc.	I live on Pong Lai Road.

Prepositions for describing our work:

at company's	I work at Comtrend
in departments	in the marketing department, **as** a technical writer.
on projects	I am working on a new manual

9. Vocabulary for common topics

The following is intended as a brief outline of some useful vocabulary for common topics that occur on the exam. For further instruction on vocabulary see my website at:

http://www.ieltsanswers.com/IELTS-Vocabulary.html

9.1. Education

Rephrasing of some common topic words:

children = juveniles, youngsters

education = learning, instruction, acquiring knowledge

students = pupils

parents = caregivers, guardians, mothers and fathers

schools = educational institutions

society = community, citizens

teachers = educators

Some useful nouns

Word	Meaning
the curriculum	the entire school program including course materials and testing of students. Everything that a school aims to teach students.
graduate	a person who has graduated from a school
illiteracy	the inability to read and write
literacy	the ability to read and write
nurture	to help grow or develop
pedagogy	the way of teaching including the instructional methods that is used
qualification	what someone gets when they graduate from school. For instance, a diploma is a qualification.
social skills	the ability to communicate and interact well with others
student centred education	a philosophy of education where the student is the central focus
tuition	the fees for studying a course

Some useful verbs

Word	Meaning
graduate	to pass a course or level of study
concentrate	to focus attention towards a particular activity, subject or problem
revise	to review materials that have already been taught
enrol	to join a class
indoctrinate	to teach following a biased belief or point of view. For example: Hitler indoctrinated young Germans with a hatred for other races.
interpret	to understand in a particular way. For example, we need to interpret the meaning of the painting.
persevere	to not give up. To keep doing something for the success is achieved.
procrastinate	to delay or put off doing something

Some useful adjectives

Word	Meaning
academic	relating to education especially universities.
co-educational	when male and female students are taught together in the same school.
single sex	when only need male or female students are taught in the same school.
hands-on	to learn by actually doing. We can get hands-on experience by actually doing things.
multi-disciplinary	involving several different subjects or areas of study.
pedagogical	relating to teaching methods and principles.
primary education	an elementary school or the first years of formal schooling.
secondary education	high school
segregated	separated. For example, the classes are segregated by gender.
tertiary education	university or vocation school
vocational	concerns teaches the skills necessary for a particular job. This concept is often applied to trade schools. So if you studying cooking or the penetration you are going to a vocational school.

9.2. Health

Rephrasing of some common topic words:

health = well-being, physical condition, fitness

healthy = fit, in good condition

unhealthy = unwell, poor medical condition

sick people = patients, people who are unwell

treatment = cure, healing

sickness = medical condition

Some useful nouns

Word	Meaning
addiction	the condition of not being unable to stop doing something. Especially something harmful like drinking alcohol or playing video games.
allergy	a strong reaction to something. For instance, an <u>allergy</u> to a certain food.
anxiety	stress
diagnosis	an opinion of a patient's health condition or illness.
diet	1. everything that we eat. 2. a plan to eat carefully to reduce weight.
insomnia	inability or difficulty to get to sleep.
ingredients	the different foods that go into a recipe.
obesity	being extremely overweight.
nutrition	the health value of food.
physician	another word for doctor.
treatment	a way of curing an illness or medical condition.

Some useful verbs

Word	Meaning
administer	to give a treatment to a patient.
counteract	to respond or act in opposition to something. For example, we need to counteract the effects of global warming.
eliminate	to get rid of something.
diagnose	to work-out what is wrong with a patient.
diet	to attempt to lose weight by eating more carefully.
prevent	to stop something happening.
stipulate	to require something. For example, the contract stipulates that you must pay your medical bill by the end the month.
trigger	to cause something to happen. For example, certain foods may trigger an allergy.

Some useful adjectives

Word	Meaning
acute	very serious
chronic	long-lasting
hazardous	very dangerous
nutritious	used to describe food that is healthy. For example, fruit and vegetables are very nutritious.
vital	very important

9.3. Media,

Rephrasing of some common topic words:

influence = effect on

negative development = harmful trend

internet = cyberspace

media = paparazzi [negative]

popularity = fame, attractiveness

Some useful nouns

Word	Meaning
a medium	medium is the singular form of media [plural].
censorship	when certain types of messages are blocked. For instance, the government often uses censorship for movies that are violent or have sexual content.
credibility	refers to whether something is reliable or from a reliable source.
exaggeration	when the truth is stretched or enlarged.
ideology	a way of thinking or belief system.
journalism	journalism is the way of reporting the news, by including newspapers, magazines, radio and television, the internet.
journalist	a person who has a career in journalism.
mass media	mass media refers collectively to all the forms of media we have such as television, radio, film, on-line services, magazines and newspapers.
propaganda	propaganda occurs the media favours certain kinds of stories or distorts messages to influence the opinions of behaviour of people.
social media	this usually refers to online tools for communication such as Facebook and Twitter.

Some useful verbs

Word	Meaning
broadcast	to send messages. For instance the TV broadcasts shows every night.
censor	to block or a strict information or content, especially when it includes violence or inappropriate content.
exploit	to take advantage of someone. For example, whenever a celebrity makes a mistake and public the media is always there to exploit the situation.
intrude	to invade or interfere with someone. For example the media often intrudes on people's privacy.
publicise	to make public.

Some useful adjectives

Word	Meaning
classical	following a well-established tradition
contemporary	Modern
cultural	relating to culture. For example, cultural awareness is being aware of someone's culture.
eclectic	not following any one system, such as traditional publishing or online publishing but selecting and using what are considered the best elements of all systems.
inspirational	motivating
monotonous	boring
passionate	intense or strong emotional feeling about something [positive]
vivid	clear

9.4. Technology

Rephrasing of some common topic words:

Recent = contemporary

Advances = developments

Improve = enhance, progress

Technology = scientific advancements

Some useful nouns

Word	Meaning
computerisation	to control a process by using a computer.
digital divide	the gap between those with easy access to information technology, and those without it.
gadget	any small piece of equipment.
innovation	a new way of doing something, or a new application of a technology.
revolution	major change in the way of doing something.
technophobe	someone who has a fear of using technology.
technophile	someone who embraces technology and uses it often.
telecommunications	technology used in the field of communications.

Some useful verbs

Word	Meaning
develop	to make or create.
envisage	to conceive or imagine an idea.
impact	to have an influence.
revolutionise	to make dramatic changes.
surpass	to exceed or overtake. For example, technology is developing so fast that it will one day surpass our ability to use it.

Some useful adjectives

Word	Meaning
computer literate	able to understand and communicate about computers.
obsolete	something that is no longer used. For example, typewriters are now obsolete.
outdated	something that is no longer up-to-date.
state-of-the-art	the latest in most recently available.
user-friendly	easy to use.
virtual	almost, especially as in almost real. For example, when we play games using virtual reality they seem like they are almost real.

9.5. Crime

Rephrasing of some common topic words:

Punishment = penalty

Crime = lawbreaking, transgression, offense

Criminal = lawbreaker, offender

Laws = regulations, rules

<u>Some useful nouns</u>

Word	Meaning
corporal punishment	to punish by physically harming the offender
capital punishment	to punish by killing the offender
community service	to spend time helping the community. For example, if a person does a minor crime they are often only punished by having to do <u>community service</u>.
consequences	the result or effect of something
deterrent	something that prevents an action
evidence	proof that the crime occurred
fine	money paid for a crime
imprisonment	to put someone in prison
legislation	laws that are made by the government
felony	a major crime
misdemeanour	a minor crime
motive	reason for doing something
prevention	stopping something from happening
victim	the person who suffers from a crime or negative event
violation	to break a rule

Some useful verbs

Word	Meaning
commit	to do something seriously wrong. for example, to <u>commit</u> murder or suicide.
convict	to judge someone as having done a crime
execute	to kill someone
incarcerate	to put someone in prison
rehabilitate	to try to help a criminal become normal again

Some useful adjectives

Word	Meaning
guilty	someone who has done something wrong
innocent	someone who has done nothing wrong
minor	not serious
major	serious

9.6. The environment

Rephrasing of some common topic words:

Environment = biosphere, ecosystem

Damage = devastation

Pollution = contamination

Problems = issues

Solutions = solving, ways to tackle

Some useful nouns

Word	Meaning
biodegradable	something that is able to decay naturally and harmlessly.
biodiversity	refers to the number and variety of plant and animal species that exist in a particular environmental area or in the world generally.
climate	the weather conditions of a region
climate change	the concept that change is occurring to the earth's climate. [Many people believe this is based on the influence of people].
deforestation	the process by which the forests are cut down.
desertification	the process by which fertile land is turned into deserts
fossil fuels	a natural fuel such as coal, gas, or oil formed over long periods of time from the remains of living organisms.
energy conservation	saving energy
environment	the place where people animals and plants live, also known as the natural world.
extinction	the complete dying out of species
habitat	a place where animals and plants live
natural resources	resources derived from the environment. For example, wood and oil.
renewable energy	describes a form of energy that can be produced as quickly as it is used, such as solar energy.

Some useful verbs

Word	Meaning
absorb	to take in something. For example, the cloth absorbed the rain.
conserve	to not waste something
deplete	to use up
diminish	to reduce something
discharge	to release something
contaminate	to make something become polluted
endanger	to put something or someone in the danger
impact	to influence
preserve	to keep something safe
retain	to keep something

Some useful adjectives

Word	Meaning
alternative	a different way of doing something
critical	extremely important
disposable	something that can be thrown away
efficient	performing or functioning in the best possible manner with the least waste of time and effort
environmentally friendly	something that is good or not harmful to the environment
hazardous	something dangerous
renewable	able to be renewed or replenished
toxic	something poisonous

10. Useful linking words and phrases

Sequencing the first idea	Adding supporting ideas	Adding a contrasting idea	Making general statements
The main reason is The most important consideration is… First of all, In the first place,	Another reason is… Furthermore, Moreover, In the same vein,	On the other hand, However, Nevertheless, Although,	As a general rule, Generally, In most cases,
Giving examples	**Giving an explanation**	**Clarifying an opinion**	**Drawing a conclusion**
For example, For instance, In particular, A clear example of this is…	The reason for this is… This is because… This is due to…	To be more precise… More specifically… By this I mean… In other words,	As a consequence, Therefore, As a result,
Stating your opinion	**Partially correct statements**	**Other people's opinions**	**Making a concession**
From my perspective, From my point of view, In my opinion	somewhat agree/disagree to a certain degree, to some extent,	From a political point of view, From the point of view of the economy, Some people believe…	It is sometimes argued that… Admittedly, However,
To give advantages	**To give disadvantages**	**To express cause**	**to express effect**
A major advantage of this is… Another important merit is… The final benefit is…	One major drawback is… Another disadvantage is… The final limitation is that…	Owing to… Due to the fact that… For the reason that…	Therefore, As a consequence, As a result…

SPECIAL OFFER

Thank you for purchasing my book and taking the time to read it. I hope that it will be beneficial and help you to achieve the score you need in the IELTS writing exam.

As a sign of appreciation I would like to offer you a free essay correction using my essay editing and correction services. In order to take advantage of this offer, please send me an e-mail of your essay and the invoice number for purchasing this book. My e-mail address is: **mike@IELTSanswers.com**

I believe it is extremely beneficial to have an experienced person read your essays and give you feedback on how to improve them. This can avoid many of the typical errors that occur on test day and help you to maximise your score.

Made in the USA
San Bernardino, CA
19 September 2015